American Presidents

Bill Clinton

by Rachel Grack

BELLWETHER MEDIA • MINNEAPOLIS, MN

Blastoff! Readers are carefully developed by literacy experts to build reading stamina and move students toward fluency by combining standards-based content with developmentally appropriate text.

 Level 1 provides the most support through repetition of high-frequency words, light text, predictable sentence patterns, and strong visual support.

 Level 2 offers early readers a bit more challenge through varied sentences, increased text load, and text-supportive special features.

 Level 3 advances early-fluent readers toward fluency through increased text load, less reliance on photos, advancing concepts, longer sentences, and more complex special features.

★ **Blastoff! Universe**

Reading Level

Grade
K

Grades
1–3

Grade
4

This edition first published in 2022 by Bellwether Media, Inc.

No part of this publication may be reproduced in whole or in part without written permission of the publisher. For information regarding permission, write to Bellwether Media, Inc., Attention: Permissions Department, 6012 Blue Circle Drive, Minnetonka, MN 55343.

Library of Congress Cataloging-in-Publication Data

Names: Koestler-Grack, Rachel A., 1973- author.
Title: Bill Clinton / by Rachel Grack.
Description: Minneapolis, MN : Bellwether Media, 2022. | Series: Blastoff! Readers: American Presidents | Includes bibliographical references and index. | Audience: Ages 5-8 | Audience: Grades 2-3 | Summary: "Relevant images match informative text in this introduction to Bill Clinton. Intended for students in kindergarten through third grade"-- Provided by publisher.
Identifiers: LCCN 2021011381 (print) | LCCN 2021011382 (ebook) | ISBN 9781644875124 (library binding) | ISBN 9781648344800 (paperback) | ISBN 9781648344206 (ebook)
Subjects: LCSH: Clinton, Bill, 1946---Juvenile literature. | Presidents--United States--Biography--Juvenile literature.
Classification: LCC E886 .G73 2022 (print) | LCC E886 (ebook) | DDC 973.929092 [B]--dc23
LC record available at https://lccn.loc.gov/2021011381
LC ebook record available at https://lccn.loc.gov/2021011382
Library of Congress Cataloging-in-Publication Data

Editor: Elizabeth Neuenfeldt   Designer: Josh Brink

Printed in the United States of America, North Mankato, MN.

Table of Contents

Who Is Bill Clinton?	4
Time in Office	12
What Bill Left Behind	20
Glossary	22
To Learn More	23
Index	24

Bill Clinton was the 42nd
president of the United States.
He served from 1993 to 2001.

Many people enjoyed
peace and **prosperity**!

Bill's Hometown

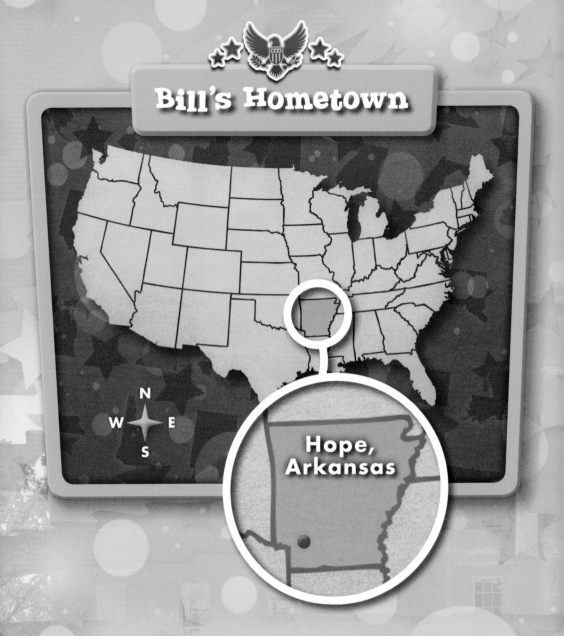

Hope,
Arkansas

N W E S

Bill was born in Hope,
Arkansas, in 1946.

In high school, he met President John F. Kennedy. This **inspired** Bill to be a **politician**!

Bill meeting John. F Kennedy

Later, Bill went to Georgetown **University**. He studied politics. He worked for an Arkansas politician, too.

Presidential Picks

Books

The Last of the Mohicans, Black Beauty, and *The Robe*

Hobbies

doing crossword puzzles and playing saxophone

Sport

golf

Foods

cheeseburgers, barbeque, cinnamon rolls, and pie

In 1970, he went to Yale Law School. He became a **lawyer**.

Afterwards, Bill went back to Arkansas. In 1978, he was **elected** as **governor**.

He worked for better schools. He also worked for a better **economy**.

Question

What helped Bill become president?

In 1992, Bill won
the presidential election.
He took office in 1993.

He wanted more **diversity** in politics. He picked women and people of color for government jobs.

Presidential Profile

Place of Birth

Hope, Arkansas

Birthday

August 19, 1946

Schooling

Georgetown University and Yale Law School

Term

1993 to 2001

Party

Democratic

Signature

Bill Clinton

Vice President

Al Gore

Bill strengthened the economy.
In 1993, he signed an agreement.
It made millions of new jobs!

Bill with French President Jacques Chirac

Bill kept peace, too.
He worked with leaders
around the world.

In 1996, Bill was reelected.
He made a new national
budget. It helped schools,
children, and families.

Bill Timeline

November 3, 1992

Bill Clinton is
elected president

March 11, 1993

Bill picks Janet Reno
as the first female U.S.
Attorney General

December 8, 1993

Bill signs the
North American
Free Trade Agreement

November 5, 1996

Bill is reelected

August 5, 1997

The Balanced Budget
Act is passed

December 19, 1998

Bill is impeached for
lying under oath

January 20, 2001

Bill leaves office

Bill was **impeached** in 1998. He lied under **oath**. But he was found not **guilty**.

He kept leading the U.S. He passed laws to help the **environment**.

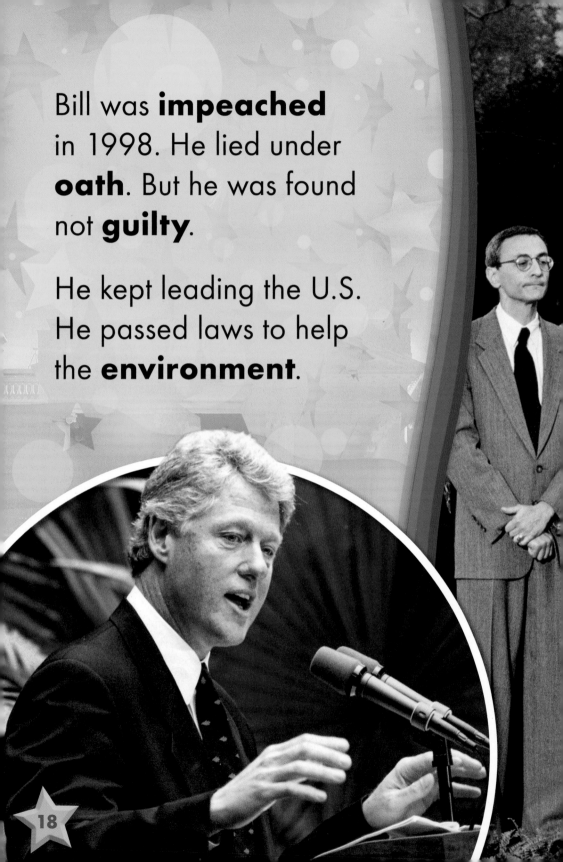

Bill left office in 2001. As president, he worked to bring peace. He helped businesses grow.

He gave hope
to many people!

Glossary

budget—a plan for how money will be raised and spent

diversity—the inclusion of people of different races, genders, and backgrounds in a group

economy—the way a state or country makes, sells, and uses goods and services

elected—chosen by voting

environment—the surrounding natural conditions that affect how living things survive

governor—the leader of the government of a state

guilty—responsible for doing something bad or wrong

impeached—charged with a crime done while in office

inspired—gave someone an idea about what to do or create

lawyer—a person trained to help people with matters relating to the law

oath—a promise to tell the truth

politician—a person who is active in government, usually as an elected official

prosperity—success, especially related to money

university—a school that people go to after high school

To Learn More

AT THE LIBRARY

Messner, Kate. *The Next President: The Unexpected Beginnings and Unwritten Future of America's Presidents.* San Francisco, Calif.: Chronicle Books, 2020.

Pettiford, Rebecca. *John F. Kennedy.* Minneapolis, Minn.: Bellwether Media, 2022.

Rustad, Martha E. H. *The President of the United States.* North Mankato, Minn.: Pebble, 2020.

ON THE WEB

FACTSURFER

Factsurfer.com gives you a safe, fun way to find more information.

1. Go to www.factsurfer.com.

2. Enter "Bill Clinton" into the search box and click 🔍.

3. Select your book cover to see a list of related content.

Index

Arkansas, 6, 8, 10

budget, 16

businesses, 20

children, 16

diversity, 13

economy, 10, 14

elected, 10, 12, 16

environment, 18

families, 16

Georgetown University, 8

governor, 10

hometown, 6

impeached, 18

jobs, 13, 14

Kennedy, John F., 7

laws, 18

lawyer, 9

oath, 18

peace, 5, 15, 20

picks, 8

politician, 7, 8

politics, 8, 13

profile, 13

question, 11

school, 7, 9, 10, 16

timeline, 17

Yale Law School, 9